FIRST GRADE US HISTORY: THE FIRST AMERICANS

SPEEDY PUBLISHING

Speedy Publishing LLC
40 E. Main St. #1156
Newark, DE 19711
www.speedypublishing.com

Paleo-Indians were the first inhabitants of North America.

Paleoamericans or Paleo-Indians is a classification term given to the first peoples who entered the American continents.

They arrived during the last Ice Age, when a land bridge connected northeastern Asia to what is now Alaska.

Paleo-Indians began to cross over from Asia at least 13,000 years ago and perhaps much earlier.

During the Paleo-Indian period all the people were nomads and got their food by hunting and gathering.

They hunted the mammoth as they went, and then as the mammoth became extinct they began to hunt buffalo instead.

The Paleo Indians also ate seeds, fruits, roots, and possibly even insects.

The Paleo-Indians used stone tools, particularly projectile points and scrapers, to hunt.

They traveled in tribes of between 20 and 50 people, carrying their belongings on their back.

Paleo-Indians sought shelter in caves, but occasionally built crude shelters from brush and animal skin.

They certainly made and used dugout canoes, they paddled across islands to reach areas where camps have been identified.

Late ice age climatic changes caused plant communities and animal populations to change.

Groups moved from place to place as preferred resources were depleted and new supplies were sought.

These Paleoamericans may later have been wiped out by or interbred with Mongoloids invading from the north.

Their name, Paleo, actually comes from the Greek word "palaios," meaning ancient.

Made in the USA
Lexington, KY
13 July 2017